Night Artillery

Poems

ANURIMA BANERJI

TSAR
Toronto

We acknowledge the support of the Canada Council for the Arts for our publishing program. We also acknowledge support from the Ontario Arts Council.

Cover art by Ramona Ramlochand

Author photograph by Ramona Ramlochand

Canadian Cataloguing in Publication Data

Banerji, Anurima
    Night artillery : poems

ISBN 0-920661-90-4

I.Title.

PS8553.A466N53 2000   C 811'.6   C00-932793-2
PR9199.3.B36N53 2000

Printed in Canada by Coach House Printing.

TSAR Publications
P. O. Box 6996, Station A
Toronto, Ontario M5W 1X7
Canada
www.candesign.com/tsarbooks

For my parents and my brother

Life's waters flow from darkness.
Search the darkness, don't run from it.
JELALUDDIN RUMI

Contents

Night Artillery

I love you as certain dark things are to be loved,
in secret, between the shadow and the soul.
PABLO NERUDA

With the shadow of my passion
have I darkened your eyes, haunter
of the depths of my gaze.
RABINDRANATH TAGORE

the libra allegories

If you are profligate, if you are pure,
You are but water mixed with dust, no more -
A drop of trembling instability

                    FARID UD-DIN ATTAR

I. MIRACLE

startle me into breath

your eyes and my tears are places without maps
only your flesh has no contours to stop me
with lips craving to speak a history of the borderless,
the bride of the muse, the salt and blood from those hands
that linger over painting and stone

I swooned a broken circle
of tangerine dust,
I came in the month of cancer
weeping you into water and pearl.

II. PROPHESY

there are no verses that wound the night
I sear you with the heat of another language

let kisses be my ghazals to your lips,
saying, I will wait until you come, eshq-e-man,
I will wait until you come with armies of love and wine
my eyes will touch you more than silhouettes of poetry
let the taste of my shadow make others mute to your mouth
let my breasts make prose in each cell of your body
let the arch of my back curve into mathnawi
where tongue turns into pen for your parchment,
and no moan can sweeten the sound
of hands crooning drupad

3

to fragments of diamond and soap
washed in the pool of your skin.

III. MYTHOS

under you I am temporary, chimeric as snow

opening raw with one kiss,
flowing over the arcs of epic and elegy,
I spoon cream into hungry fingers,
cupped hands fleshed into patient lilt and thrust

I forgave you the marks of colony,
I forgave those jeweled daughters
of immigrant wind becoming war

and apart from you , I am the searcher of origins,
the mimic, the monkey, the mirror,
the cruel searcher, the knowing searcher, the dark searcher,
the hidden, the mad, the numb

keeper
of my
origins.

IV. ORACLE

tell me
about the massacre of roots

while you enter and exit
the rooms of my body,
like a homeless phantom
unearthing a palace,

a faint child of surfaces

4

in this native asylum

tell me
about the measure of love and ruin

V. REVELATION

my gaze is your private omen
a call to prayer in this orgy of light,

stripped of my lungs and orifice

I am no longer that poem

> if I cannot have you,
> soaked in dust before me
> if I cannot have you,
> melting into storm before me
> if I cannot have you,
> coiled into darkness
> before me

> I shall memorize the survival of scars
> on your wrists,
> flecks of gold chiarascuro
> blade to blade, beseeching your back,
> I shall remember a continent of oil and rock
> in the sad smiles of your brow,
> I shall chase sinew and organ,
> the ropes, bonds, and ligaments,
> breaking into pulp,
> I shall follow the sketch of your veins
> like roads into viscera
> I shall rob your whispers, the ballad of my
> soul
> I shall write you deep into the cinnamon
> bark of wood,

5

and I shall read you into my lines of treason and desire,

disrobed and failing, I shall read

I Have Your Body for Proof

1.
I have your body
for proof

of where I have
gone, what has
been lost, who has
claimed me, who has
spoken and grieved,
who has taken the past
this story beloved, who
has held me hostage
to tomorrow, who has
witnessed the swallowing
of swamps, who has sculpted
nail on nude thigh, who has
placed a hand beneath
my breast, who has
sucked limes and
honey from skin,

I have your body
for proof

2.
 These are
surfaces
I learn,

your gestures,
a private choreography,
an unpublic heartbeat,
voluptuous with
the weight of
mystery, a movement,
slow and leaking,
in sealed, permanent
grief, a movement
from the time I tried to
inhabit you,

love you from
the inside out

3.
To memorize an atlas intimately

as spirals on fingertips,
creases on lips,
to make origin unfamiliar,
to breathe the knowledge
of a thousand paper limbs,
reveal each curve or speed
she travelled.
I am still waiting for signs
of you, passion muted
by silence. Make me
an articulate lover.
Let me find you again
like this: darkly, nightly,
asylumed from sleep, paused
like water, dense air and age.
let me find you again, under the sheets
of our beds, in letters and paper,
desire and voice - return, where

I have only your body
for proof.

Anjali

a late inscription:

I will hunt your absence
the shade and harvest, rhythm and branch
the water in my belly full of
your name, a hunger that stabs

struck, I cannot breathe
or lie about your image,
savage in me. these poems
open with words, dividing
and multiplying in the path
of your blood, then swelling
on a dark page.

come to my mouth, and give me
incantations, lost without you
to speak them into being.
come to my mouth, and bless me,
lost without you
to speak me into being

clean my hair of thorns

take handfuls
of salt and incense, oil and smoke,
hidden perfumes in the aura of skin.
search the strange prism
of my veins

touch my hands, arrows
stolen from night's artillery,

love

tinged lapis, sky, indigo

Shanti Jal

Let water wash over
her palms

the autumn of my heart
has turned leaf to golden ochre
and the ruse of the murmur
has hardened into stone.
memory turns in cycles and loops,
mirror, ocean, mimesis

she is spilling, crashing,
then cracking
into bones
and I mix blood with the roots
to make her grow into poems
planted in another country

like an anchor she holds me,
drifting, serene, a shell caught on waves,
tearing through the skin of time zones
until the surface of the temporary
becomes the subject of our lives
until the ephemeral world has
the sharper silhouette

and I am sinking in her arms

I was born in the country of mud,
padmini, swamps,
stark, uncertain, alone
and now, trapped in a skeleton
flesh made blue from the inside
I turn sapphire, body twisting
into violet archipelago

we have shed islands, nations, masks

myths that were never ours,
the terror of return,
and only for her I wait
with open palms

this line of desire
is sometimes too far, too remote
measured fine like diamond dust
pieces of you
splintered in my hands

a secret eye, the birth
of fire from your lip,
lethal, leaping across continents of skin,
brass, alabaster, gold,
a true mosaic, shapes of glass,
a portrait
of my broken body

frozen at the edge of fault lines
where she closed her eyes
and gave me a libretto:
the alphabet of tears
trickling down
at the tender cusp
of her palms

Swallowing the Remains

I came to hang myself
in your tree
at the threshold of
leaves and flowers

I fell under the wheels

of a rickshaw
scarred my forehead, tore my knees,
crushed my elbows into the ground.

I molded the cup of your hands
to be the strong one
underneath,
arms held at half-mast,
clasped around
my faded replica of love.

I imagined you were
a cave of thin bones
versus the weight
of   cylinders.

Three lives later

condemning my body
to know what stays below
the surface of things,
I asked you to come, listen
for the bells.

And this is what I said:

*to love is to swallow
another's remains,
to love is to wade through
liquid and trenches,
while bodies are spellbound,
cold and exposed, water
in pools at the collarbone.*

You lowered your eyes
before the streets
lost their lights.

Sleeping Rumour

...sleeping like the rumour of a pearl
in the embrace of oysters.
                    MICHAEL ONDAATJE

I am travelling
where the ice falls
and stabs,

holding my light
in the tempo of blood

burning snow
to extinguish
the hour of saturn

you pearled me
into the hands of a history
that lies,
the hollowed flesh and lesion

later, you will leave scars.

there is nothing now that reminds me,
nothing,
that my skin was only a map
stretched for bruised eyes,
the evidence of knives,
signs that you have come
and gone.

there is nothing now
no alpana of saffron stains,
nothing of those circles on my neck
turning your private hunger
into public name

12

make me new, then
from raw blood,
dust and footprint, night and water

all that composes and remains

a spell, an angel, an empty glass,
my sleeping   rumour   of   love.

Madhur

like a secret smile at midnight
in the heart of my palm

you come (soft) through orphaned magenta
through marble veins and muscle

your heat dares to escape my sighs
as you slip into steam

and offer a bitter enigma
troubled by water i rose into blood

becoming the moon's assassin
you smuggle scarlet into ephemeral

trembling and speechless, i stand

mulaqat

with a mirror of breath   you stole my body   from its roots
this urgent ritual of flesh   pulls me into your depths
nomad wandering   through borders of bone   i have no home
but your woman's body   living between curves   of shoulder
and breast   head inside   the temple of your thighs
lush tresses of skin   unfold secrets   into beauty
lover   we have tongues tied   to memory of scars
floating in oracles   seeking oaths   of origin and allegiance
we cross the waters   and enter   each other's bodies
giving new incarnations   perpetual synchronicity
making a pilgrimage   of desire   sung to love

rati

i am swallowed by the tongue of night her
fist buried deep beneath bruises these quiet
purples and blues screaming red gently rocking
her moan on my lips i travel to the country of
breasts with its boundary of flesh covering
her remote heart of bone disintegrating dark
pauses all tremors locked in her limbs
her fragrance drowning my body in
fluid melodies of grace of earth of shells
breaking sound silence streaming auras

open your eyes from blackness as you swim
into surrender of crimson touched raw
tasting love this love my love yes love
we love and love

14

Mashuqa

This body needs gestures. All tongues are omens. Kisses. Snow crushed into quartz. Pressed flowers, pulled from the thighs of books. A triangle of scent. Beyond her, a sheath of prayer. The arms of the beloved, the arms of longing. A slur of light. Low fire. Paper lanterns. Blue music of flames, in decrescendo. Then an echo: sound repeating sound forgetting itself. She is a spy, stealing treasure. After the hour of nameless ritual has passed.

The gift of another. The opening of lips. Falling into caverns, spilling out of edges and lines, leaning over the precipice. A robe of hair, undone. A turn of wrist, undressed. Eyelids closing, moist, under lashes like fans, a film of tears. Fluid, liquid, shapeless. A body cascades, caught in deluge, mercury trapped in stone. Blood as libation. A nail on a ring, a hand in a circle, a palm of spirals. Inside, a tulip of flesh. Tearing at palisades, a thin lacuna of membrane. The tulip of flesh, split. The lagoon filling with milk, her last offering. Hauntings of the place of secretions, a taste, emissions from the place of beginnings, another taste. Shoulders, dunes, elbows, cities, neck, corner, stop.

Breath, hands, eyes. Mirrors of teal. Glass body glass. Shaking, slipping out of fingers, out of reach, crash. Light tumbles through half-opened doors, falters through prisms of skin pure with light. A slant of wood under footprints, aching against the bed. Touching frost. An early courtship of silver and maroon. Marbles wet with moonlight, scattered by her feet. Her fingers streaked gold: hidden underwater, she tastes gold. Then. A garnet of blood, the prize of conquer on her thumb. She is empty. Later, there is more gold and liquid crystal, the magic of her alchemy.

Fade to speech, fade to dark.

15

Raga Malkauns

alap.

her skin unfurls like a scroll of papyrus

        intimately she whispers her prayers into my skin
          inscribing the secrets of sanskrit with on my hips

and there is the calligraphy of her tongue
this woman's ink brushed into every pore

        she is waiting for the woman
        who promises to be her muse, while

the shape of apples lingers in my hands

jor.

wrapped in auburn sheets of sky,
I listen to her prison of solitude

        she does not see with her eyes:
        it is her hands that have the gift of sight

her fingers skilled in the subtle lines
between noon and dusk, nuances of shade
lying between azure and turquoise

jhala.

I have waited for her these centuries
while my skin turned from gold to grey
I waited through my senseless days

        (I waited for you, becoming the salt desert
        drained of a mellow sea)

and when the ocean parts
her thighs
when I move
into the red tide
you will step
from my shoulders
to the peninsula
you will walk on the prickly bones
of my spine
to genesis
and send me bloated kisses
until I breathe

The Story of Chrysanthemums

miracles are not always temporary. another wonder, your eyes.
arms momentarily still. and i, quiet, before you reach out
to trace pale moons around my delicate shadow. midnight,
cloudless and moist, wraps me in its hundred wet limbs,
searching for cool flesh to subdue the calloused stillness.
even as you close your eyes for sleep dreaming itself
through the beauty of your body. begin the visitation without me.
sleep into days burnished by noon, shallow with twilight,
obsidian nights. sleep in the orbit of heartbeat.

then, it is your body, slipping from tongues of unnamed ice,
under the hennaed prints of my first blood. your body against
a dervish of flame. black-eyed, having hunted your love,
i am vermillion prisoned in the mist of your thighs.

In the Year of Aquarius

There is a kind of pressure in humans to take whatever
       is most beloved by them
and smash it

                                   ANNE CARSON

the other flesh

I entered, a transparent
chameleon, gliding across the miles
of your face.
you seeped into my body,
intimate as habit

into my other flesh
you came, your hand
cupping my hand,
shoulder brushing shoulder

you lift me, and I am
tangled beneath, light
as chiffon and sheer
with love, so thin
that layers and layers
will not protect me
from tearing

necessary love:
like bread and breath.
you leave. and this is
the pattern of our lives,
the common thing
embroidered between us:

you leave, and I embrace
what is left behind

the flood of sighs in sleep,
deep rhythms at night,
your body, part of familiar
language, native to my tongue,
something I know
before anything else.

but we are purest
in our separate
selves,
no masquerade of
joining at each cave,
shell-smooth, bone-cold.

and we make lies, not love
finding strange eyes
lit across foreign rooms,
music from a red distance.

you sit, perfect and porcelain,
while I am the one about to break,
your curled fist smashing my palms
echoless.

I feel the palest phase of pleasure,
when I ask you to steal me
but you remain that dark statue
poised for silence

lonely, an amateur at speech,
I wonder what made you look
this way, at a prize among trophies,
girl among women. you watch
my lyrics crumble.

all I see around here
is someone else's. you
are someone else's.
nothing, nothing is mine.

waiting around the corner
of the map, to fall
in love, you were too late
for passion's crime.
and in leaving, you would turn,

. is the root of blood
and I,
your other flesh.

Heart Murmurs

Montreal train station—
where those who are loved
disappear on slow tracks—
this is the place where we meet again.

Waiting for you, I am caught
in the crowd's tableau:

A man reads the schedule,
entranced, as if it is a thriller,
filled with all the suspense
of arrivals and departures.
A woman sits alone at the fast
food table, pouring coffee
into a plastic cup with fingers
thin and trembling. Another poses
calmly with a drink of tea.
A father and daughter pause
to embrace.

And I look past them, for you,
as soft and nervous as a snail.

You arrive abruptly
through a breach of light,
for a kiss in the afternoon's small symphony,
emblems of rain on your sleeve.
Your body,
bound in lithe black cotton,
moves   curves   sprints
through stories of lovers
into the next scene:

                      an empty room, scattered with our pictures.

I am in love. Not with you,
but a moment composed
from the silence of minutes,
the iris of an amber eye
glazed in winter light. there is
nothing else as fragile to hold.

You speak of cancer
slicing the breath
of your lungs.

Love, I have dreams
of girls and kerosene,
women on fire in the kitchen,
wives singed by orange flames,
but nothing to equal this.

I imagine you curled into a fist
of sleep, dying in a crevice of stones,
smelling of gunpowder
or talcum.

Now my heart murmurs,
you haven't died, you haven't died,
stranger floating mortal
to earth.

And I remember standing
on the anonymous platform, filigreed
with a necklace of voices, and I hear
your hands among them, leaning for touch,
for my bare and speechless shoulders.
I catch the perfect emerald teardrops
in your eyes, even when you have forgotten
the sound of my stare.

The train is about to leave, yes.
I stop staring. I do not tell you
about the sentence coming into language
on my lips. I never finish whispering,

hide me from the world.
I want to become a snail
clasped in your palms,
shelled from touch, and still tender.

We never finish speaking of found truths.

After Half-Girl

I have killed the demon of my tongue
uttering your name, forgetting what brought us
here, a compass and oceans and boats,
desert and limestone, light against light, the dark lip
dazzled into tear, time made of libido and speed,
rooms vast and hungry with music. your name carved
into each brush of bone. there is no place for anything
else no place for anyone else nothing to announce another
into being. only the morning splitting green with grass,
poison scratch marks on my knees, secret side of a falling
body, the cold december staircase, where we made love

to cobras and violins, where you found the streets of ruin,
straying into the body of the half-girl.

Dance Lessons

After marriage you stopped dancing,
throwing music to deep ravines and crows.
Even older than I remember—
at this age, suddenly, you have a new
love for tangos.

So we dance tonight, tracing each other's insignia:
I have no ruins from children
but my hips cradle webs of stretch marks
from when I left Odissi
and you have thin knots of scars,
charting a voyage on the sea of your back.

Each mark came
from swimming in bones
and bowls of shells,
glass and paper cracked
on frail skin.

Shatter from nothing
but love
and other magic swords.
Crash, but don't leave
in darkness, exit after
the theater lights are on,
and you have perfected
the pleasure of each solo

(Your wife's eye opens
from slumber, reaching for

your arm too late, her keen visage
caught in a single column of light,
lumescent and beautiful,

her ballet of kisses
never touching your face)

Plums

i lie down in the quiet sauna,
with wet and glistening limbs,
trickling with the pure heat of water and steam.

ripened, you say, *shining small and dark as plums.*

The Sound of a Heart Cracking

I stalk you, following
imprints of your hand
engraved in stones
of a city underground.

I've been searching for you
in strange passages, in unknown
quarters, seeking your whisper in poems,
your stare in photographs, your murmurs
in rainfall. The way you stroke the line
of my limbs, supple and splendid,
spin me through revolutions
of desire I can find nowhere else.

27

These are early rehearsals for mortality,
for falling. Now the dogs have taken shreds
of my skin to feed on,
my days are spent scavenging for scraps
of your memory.

I crave any simple ritual:

> snapshots of a fist   against my jaw
> scenes of   urgent laughter
>   the sound of a heart   cracking

2. *Absence of Injury*

She doesn't suffer
wrapped
in the comfort of your gaze
She has no injury
or lie to live with

> (that she knows of)

I have a picture
of her stubborn smile,
the one that dares me
to ask you,

> "Leave her"

then falter.

There is nothing between you that will decay.

She has that safe, extravagant calm
of someone who is married,

officially, predictably
yours.

3. *This Is How I Have a Picture of Your Love*

This is how I have a picture of your love.

Ten years, a reason for my jealousy.
Ten years, of

> you in a blue robe
> on a love seat, with her at your side,
> drinking coffee in the morning,
> watching the news on television,
> then the sweetly suburban goodbyes,
> (a kiss on her cheek, a kiss on her lips)
> you drive on the freeway to go to work
> in the bank, the respectable grey building,
> and you call each other at lunchtime,
> just to see how things are, and things are always
> just fine, then you drive back home before rush hour,
> and she cooks while you clean
> you clean while she cooks.
> you turn off the lights. unplug the phone.
> then, you lock the doors.

I have memorized
each corner
of your home,
the apartment
that holds
domesticity
like a strangler.

> I know your modest portraits and paintings,
> decorative bath bubbles in pretty pink jars,
> bottles of perfume arranged carefully
> on newly dusted shelves,
> ambitious lists of groceries and cleaning agents,
> things that need to be fixed, coffee tables lined with
> the literature of management.

29

4. *You Know You Love Her*

And then there is the bedroom.

She tells you she loves you
You know you love her
She tells you she loves you
and you know you love her

You promise her she will never be hurt
But you keep that secret hidden
from me.

5. *The Perfect Marriage*

You have kissed her hands
a thousand times
You have made love to her
in nightly confessions

You were the first woman she fell in love with
and you are the last one she loves,

You have the perfect marriage.

> the walls are shrinking so tight, but
> you wanted such mathematical security,
> the deliberate precision of numbers,
> and that is what you have:
>
> a passion for the familiar.

You believe in this practice of intimacy

> so you know the exact shade
> of her favourite lipstick, the size
> of each breast, the slight rasp of her
> breath in sleep, the squeeze of her hand

30

and you know you will never, ever
leave.

6. *Something You Forget*

Years from now, when time has trampled over me
You will still sit quietly near her, glancing full of love
Profoundly lacking sensation.
But you welcome that cruelty

And curious, you will look at me
Like an animal you have killed
by accident.

There is no remorse, only pity.
Something you forget
because it never mattered.

7. *You Will Never Leave*

Repetitions can lull you.

I love you I love you I love you
I am insane to love you

You attack and disappear.

You say you haven't changed in years,
and I believe that
you have not changed since
she made you
hers

You have the perfect marriage

You were the first woman she fell in love with,
the last one she loves

31

And although you hear
the sound of my heart   cracking

You know you will never, ever

leave.

Keep Me Here

I feel the intimacy between you
and her, the way I sense age
in old cities, layers and layers
of time that have collected between
the bricks of your lives, the wars
fought along fences and borders,
history caught in the trenches, surrendering
each half of the couple, shards and measures
from memory's lines.

and I can barely hold
the weight of my own body
any longer. Drag myself out of this
old city. Punch the years out
of these bricks. Don't keep me here.
Keep me here, I asked you,
though sometimes my voice failed
to hold you,

love, my voice failed. I leave my broken
mosaic of laughter. Alone in your dead city.
I had thought I would follow your twin shadows,
make them my own private islands to inhabit.
I had thought of burning each season
suffused with the scent of your lovemaking,

then watch you fall,
protected from the rain of ashes.

In the Lebanese Cafe, 1 am

your absence is translucent.
i have been speaking in metaphor too long.
there is a memory of your presence,
mute ghost i cannot answer
through the mundane act of licking
paper with pen. if i were to photograph this,
i would frame your hand tightening
around the loneliness i take into my mouth
every night, trapped and crushed by fog,
unused to the blurred lines of the image,
aching to burn a reason for this: your slightest touch
(like ee cummings) in the cinema air, your faintest voice,
but i am only a prostitute, begging to buy you
with stale words and dry love.

still, your absence is translucent.

In the Year of Aquarius

i have an image of early paths into san francisco, and you in a boyish self,
diving off berkeley's edge. how i know you: starving for some tracks that
might mark another place, so you take the rapid transit beneath the surf,
mixing water with your poems.

later, i refused to drive across the bay bridge to see you, refused this arch
that split open during the last earthquake: my trust saved for
something else, something that would not fail in its engineering to hold us

together, in case of deeper unsettlings: we are too tenuous. i
said i would take the tunnel instead. you said there were no fish. i wanted
to be different though i never was. i had a separate vision of my underwater,
divided

from what you told me first,
standing with ice chilling a tall crystal glass, held against hot shoulders, your
throat lined with fine bones, mouth open for my fictions, all exposed to the
sun's sharp eye.

throwing my head back, i would
not believe you. i only thought of leaving the earth's surface to travel deeper
into your water's veins, following the smooth dip of the train into a world

of fish. i imagined looking out of the transparent
shield, face slanted against blue glass, gazing into the mirror of a thousand
years, searching for what has happened

without you

and i
chose not to remember that here, there is an absence of light, an absolute
cavern, an empty aquarium. shocked by speed, i did not even sense when i
rose through the spirals, without any hint of a cobalt glimpse.

afterwards, i climbed out of stupor and cried. a surprised
glance from others, like you, who knew even more than patience, who had
no prophecy of meeting with fish: but my faith cannot stay neutral.

each time i am lowered into ocean, to visit your
side of things, i harbour dangerous secrets, wishing that saltwater would
burst and open the thin tube connecting bay to bay, city with city, a saltwater
purple with quiet rage,

burning all angles of silence. and how i
wish you would never open your green eyes to anything else but my face,
the descent into your arms, my liquid hope, of floating and finding
splendors like starfish and sharks and drifting kelp,

cushioned by calm looks from sea
creatures, despite any disturbance. nothing like this happened. you did not
stay. with me. and as the train disappeared with a subtle curve, i thought i
would see such beautiful things, thought i had entered underwater grace.

and as in love, nothing
happened. roaming for your touch, alone, mesmerized by dark, all i heard
was that pressured sound, all i saw was that absence of light, and you were
nowhere,

nowhere,

lifting me out of aquamarine. you had spoken about the absence of light,
and i had not believed. now your stare impales the lie of water. i swim
through these pierced teal voids, escaping all faultlines: ready for stronger
illusions, a softer mirage.

Bending Towards Exile

somebody calls you home
night after night   then never again
ADRIENNE RICH

Hysteries for My Mother

Mother, one stone is wedged across the hole in our history
and sealed with blood wax.
In this hole is our side of the story...

It is the half that has never been told,
and some of us must tell it.

LORNA GOODISON

mother, one stone

1. mother: i know how strange that word is
i have squeezed it with my bare hands,
listening for the drone of prayer inside
i know how strange the word is, mother,
you, a stone without history

and i have no feeling for this stone in my stomach
about to soften and scream, like cancer
a distant killer
growing and bleeding inside
that is how i give birth to children
i have no feeling, mother, but fear
for what i was, a cyst,
the size of marbles,
and you held me back
with the shell of milk and membrane

afraid of this cyst, mother,
that later burst into a daughter
shaped around a list of years,
our nameless talismans
of failure

sealed with blood wax

2. and you are crying, mother
because i turned away

not a daughter   but shame

a daughter for a mother
(that strange word)
swollen with a love that knows
only the detail of what passes through
man and woman,

not the bone i have brought
from her, or the eye, watching
you from the inside,
a moving carapace of flesh

that stone filled with shame
and lining my stomach,
mother, that stone is yours

                                                        the hole in our history
(midilogue)

my mother is a hundred
other mothers. she is betrayed,
or alien. she drapes saris at home,
one piece of gauzy cloth spun
around her like a beautiful bandage.
for the broken butterfly. soon, for work,
she slips into awkward shrouds
lamenting pieces of her body—
blue jacket for shoulders and arms,
full skirt for waist and hips, sheer
pantyhose for legs. each limb divided
on this doll, a smile stuck to the face.

like a difficult pregnancy, her face
is full of complications. mother and girl.
we stand in the kitchen, performing identical
tasks —placing teacups in the cupboard —

unable to look at one another. a limb
divided. when our glances collide, my face
is not her child's, but a difficult daughter's,
another awkward piece of her body that
later needed bandage. we hold still in the dark
kitchen, each with teacup shaking in hand—

a universe apart, eye to eye,
the road between our stares
paved with loss and distance.

our side of the story

3. mother, in your pictures you are young
you have memory
but nostalgia is the mark of age:
the exact measure between
the fulfillment of desire
and its disappointment.

i have seen fear crumble
when decay begins. i have seen your
fugitive hands, and open fingers
fleeing suspicion

you are soundless in sleep, mother,
waiting for the arms of death
to lift you, thin as light
and tentative

my mother's seclusion,
the bomb waiting to explode.

has never been told

4. mother, you are my red blade
of concubine tongue
walking in the eclipse of lost souls,

41

the ache of half-frozen fingers
trembled on a broken string

mother, when your blue hands
stroked zari and thread
did your eyes sing bhairavi?
pluck the notes of craving
with tears? did your eyes
conquer peaches and apples,
fields of mustard and wheat in his body?
did your eyes make my father shy
and foreign? did your eyes heed love,
the call to malkauns?

when, mother, did your eyes
sing?

Merge

for my father

Babi, I am your mapmaker, the holder of
your atlas, the messenger of destination
or beginning. We are new cartographers,
shrinking California into simple dots with
squares, marking artery roads to the heart
of the myth.

Babi, you never allowed me to give directions.
You refuse to trust signs, locks, neon lights,
all the things that sometimes show the way.

And you would not let me drown where I wanted.
You would not have me lie with strangers. You could not
see me leap out of planes, crash into cars. You would
not make me drive or swerve.

The theories of separation and distance are what
you know best. Circles are enigmas, but
you engineer infinities of parallels, eternal
sequences of perpendiculars, points of momentary
intersection. Suspicious of parabola,
a surgeon of angles and radius,
no dangerous curves, you measure intimacies
in diagonals, straight lines that cut across but
do not join. Stay their own.

Stay your own, you said,
keen on the special effects of math,
lessons from love's biography. This
is what you taught me, always,

do not merge.

bending towards exile

condition iii ensures that the velocity vectors
along the images of coordinate curves are
everywhere linearly independent.

bending towards exile - I have lost the
home that housed my childhood and bitterly
looking inside, wanting to touch your walls
defiled by the robber devaki told me about
I do not remember
fragments of glass pieced along bricks to bleed
any trespasser into my memory
I stared at you, as if expecting
you to wait, and your emptiness
confirmed mine. I remembered
things I never wanted to leave and when
I see you I want to fill you with my
symbols. you conform to the past
I have made for myself

and she remembers all the childhood
stored in the soil beneath foundation
it is as if you were mine and I need
to possess the bittersweet delhi days
gone since the trauma of planes
placed us two, three, four continents away
schizophrenia still has not left me

no other house has made me its own since
yes, I have admired the erotics of space
another freedom allows,
wooden floors and functional furniture
simple architectures of the outside
but I imagine you as a home with peacocks and lizards
all the animals nursed in your confines
home, incarceration, extracted through violence.

what does it mean, that I return to
devastations of noise? dispossessed, my language
means nothing, as if you put me into
exile, from owning the deepest parts
of myself. delhi's sun, delhi's streets, yes mir,
every scene is like a painting and work
of art.

I am betrayed and relieved by
the lack of life inside you - the insolence
in loneliness, without claiming me as
the body of your territory
translating house into flesh from mortar
and brick. transactions of space into movement.
I am grateful that no one has taken you
made you their own beyond my consent.

when did what you arouse become so simple?
am I so immune from roots,
protected from the stability of our usual
prisons, four walls, closed doors, concrete foundations
that cannot disintegrate? no, my contours
have been deformed. fragments define me now.
divisions, partitions, reclamations
are my history, the asymmetrical
geography of my heart. this silence

of your frame still haunts me
even as i went to the splendour of
the taj and sought to write poetry about
you instead. why? in place of tears,
there are words
to expel you on the violence
of the page.

you may still be familiar but
we have changed and neither of us
stopped growing that desire

for belonging. I carried you with me
across all the fixity, the boundaries
unspoken. your memory ceases
to become linear, rather there are collages,
and pastiche, a cornucopia of riches
swimming the chaos

what genre can I write you into?
nothing else is adequate, except the
immediate imposition of
poetry
to contain you.

is there ever a return from exile,
time punctured before you can claim it?

the accident of migration has made me more beautiful,
less myself, love quantified into a commodity of remembrance.

Air India, June 1985

under the camouflage of waves i came to hear you,
flying sky to earth for water. you washed me in
marigold tears, caught against the belly of cyclones
before you could offer blessing. and i thought of you
that split second i spilled onto rocks between
the twin sides of my heart, between worlds I learned
to love, not dread, body resting and cleansed now
by the sea. I see you standing, finite and exiled, familiar
with kumkum, tremble, and mangalsutra, waves ringing
in my spine, when the call of the conch shell
meets the three worlds.

Elegy for June

tonight

I cradle loneliness
like a half-wept child
without lullabies,

then send photographs
to strangers with broken faces

I write letters to amnesia
with your ashes

but come, look,
there is unforgetting
in our blood, you will not leave

here are the hundred places
where I find you,

here is your heart
painted on the blue skin
of nostalgia

and I still keep your eyes
on my wrists,
unfolding these hands

to open a poet's dream
for the blind and living

47

She Was Never a Prisoner

Her best friend is beside her
in snapshots from Disneyland,
pictures of swing sets and suburban
houses. Barbecues in the backyard.
Swimming at the lake in summer.

There are fights that last the whole day,
cuts and scratches, twisted ankles, broken arms,
the shape of what is to come.

She can smash her cheek and kiss it.

She can smash her cheek and kiss it, too.
This is how she learns what love is:
a white bone punished into bruise, liquid
pink and congealed, a painting paralyzed
on the face, numbed shock, hushed squeal.
The heart waiting for repair, forgotten,
the skin's ridge cleaved and healed,
sealing the proof of damage. Forgiveness
pulled through the minor act of a kiss.

This is how she learns what love is

They are always together. Always the same.
This is what she thinks.

She doesn't want to lose her to the boys.

But she has lost her friend to the boys,
the boys who kiss her
and bite her
and chase her
the boys who didn't know any better,
because they were boys,
stupid, muscled boys

She did lose her to the boys,
the boys who opened her legs
by force
(because they were family)
the boys who didn't know how
to tell truth from shame,
the boys who sent her love notes
calling her *bitch*.

She lost her to the boys.

She loves her best friend still,
the lack of ambiguity in her mouth,
rough eyes, skin dark, lips tight,
the tongue she once sucked like a lollipop
all one before the boys came.

Now, her friend says she'll break
those boys' jaws and ribs,
burn them with cigarettes
when they threaten to kill her
because they can't.

But her body is wrecked from the knife
of a husband. When everything fell,
she stayed. When everything broke, she
did not leave. It takes her too long to realize
that love is not a duty to men
just because they are.

And it takes her too long to see
that love can die, that sometimes you have
to kill it, that murder is not always a crime
or a choice, that you don't stay alive just because
you have so far survived.

And it would not take her long
to bring another stupid, muscled

49

boy back into her bed
because she's lonely
and they're not half as strong.

She is still tough and pretty,
living in a shell of glass,
shards in her spine, splinters on her back.
The window is shattered with his gift
of gunshot, brick, and bottle.
She is locked behind a door,
shouting back against his slaps,
his greedy fingers.

It's been years that she has hunched over
food in the kitchen, chopping with a cleaver,
her neck slouched, her hands raw
from age and defiance.

This is the woman I love,
the one stripped down to the bone
of who she is,
the one I lost to the boys.
She looks at me sometimes,
in a picture frame on the dresser
where she keeps her private things.

At least, that's what she tells me,
but I know our lives are lies.

We are far away from who we were,
and closer and closer to learned love -
the pummelled cheek, the line of damage
showing the place where the body's seams
have come apart, time suturing the wound
back into a face that cannot forget. We are
learning that love is exactly the same as when
we were children.

Shocked bone, hushed squeal, numb kiss.
And the heart always waiting for repair.

Passage to India

this is no karma queen
        indian princess
                brown sugar
                        exotic beauty
                                sapno ki rani

this is no rajasthani
        miniature painting
                pining milkmaid
                        with doe eyes and peacock gait

this is no heavy-breasted
        honey-skinned
                large-hipped
                        rose-lipped
                                goddess

these are no devi's
        lotus-blossom cheeks
                tresses spilled to waist
                        kajal-decorated gaze
                                red bindi
                                        hands of mehndi
                                              payal tinkling on her feet

this is no sati-savitri
        sita in fire ordeal
                radha longing for krishna

this is no virgin actress

turning face before kiss
    with coy tilt of head
        shy of gaze

this is no air india hostess
    hands folded in namaste
        bearing rose garlands
            "welcome to india"

this is no desi dasi
    cooking your curry
        making your chai
            and rasmalai

this is no arranged marriage bride
    in red and gold benarasi sari
        seeking your ashirbad

this is no sensual, spiritual, east-meets-west

this is no incense-burning
    sweet-smelling
        ripe courtesan

no soft kamala for siddhartha
    well-versed in pleasure
        with tongue of silk
            chanting a mantra or
                reading a chakra

this is no sandalwood-scented lover
    spice girl singing ragas
        to sitar and tabla
            dancer of haunting
                lyric and melody

this is no stanadayini, breast-giver
    no swollen clit dripping rosewater cunt juice

                    orgasmic ecstatic tantric liberation
                  exotic erotic kama sutra vulva
                    opening her divine legs
                              mysterious oriental fantasy
                                        come to life

yes, i have a cobra tongue
                          and my third eye will strike

but no
              my vagina is not
                              the passage to india

Summer

or,

I Want the Rage of Poets to Bleed Guns
Speechless with Words

I. Summer is the season of sun

and rape. tanning: I am not thinking of a leisurely afternoon on the riviera
with bronzing cream but tanning, like an animal slaughtered, bodies packed
into ice like meat, torn skin
ripped
from bone, stretched wide across grass, something like a hammer pounding
leather (dead).

This is me, Draupadi: I am thinking of a hand as soft as darkness, I am
thinking of murmurs and kissing, the burden of a body under the weight of
rebellion. With eyes
like guillotines, I carry the impression of footprints she walked that day, out
the door, downstairs, against the wall where she pressed my thighs and

53

kissed—

and I am thinking of an ambulance, police cars, the mythology of birth, him,
that terror on the highway, the street, and at home.

It has been this way for a long time, since they put a restraining order against
my breasts and called it a bra.

—Were you wearing something provocative?
—No
—Were you wearing something provocative?
—No
—Were you wearing something provocative?
—Yes, my vagina

II. Chandrabhaga

where does the sun begin or my body end (bloody)

between the cries of *bitch, pussy, fuck*
in this summer, season of crime
I am a traitor to semen in this season of
gun
held in mouth like I should come to him while he comes in me
but I am a traitor, a dyke, crawling out of light like a cockroach
or just like a cock, and he's got his gun cocked in my mouth
about to burst until

I bleed guns speechless with words

III. this is what makes me live: pierced nipples

and gauze, a look that brings me
to my knees,

54

when I want it

Do you understand?

When I want it
from her

IV. I will make amerika sink
this is my motherfucking country
and tonight

between my sheets,
I am making love and slow jazz
with a woman slipping through sweat
and nightmare,
sliding into the hard grace
of thighs clenched like fists
that smashed my jaw that day,
but he could not strip words
out of me, they come back
virus

until I bleed guns speechless

V. living in the body of a poet in vertigo,
          she rolls syllables off her tongue,

satyam shivam sundaram.

                    om bhur bhuvaha swaha
                    tat savitur varenyam
                    bhargo devasya dhimahi
                    dhiyoyonaha prachodayaat.

In the beginning of this poem she finds me,

55

om namah saraswate
om namah durge
om namah kali
om namah stute.

And skin to skin,
this is satyam shivam sundaram,
sruti and smriti,
the prayer of wedding
never uttered outside
man and woman

these are small pieces of longing I write,
with more devotion than veda or darshan,
words thicker than the smoke
rising from the stripped scalp of coconut
in the morning.

VI Surya:

I could not tell you where water ends and her body begins

there is no other way to know this, only
travel through sinew and muscle,
through ventricle and chamber,
through marrow, bone, and blood—

VII. *love, I heard you underneath*

like Vishnu crawling seas as fish,
Buddha in samadhi,
Krishna smashing body against soul,

satyam shivam sundaram.

she saw me in the making of death, and I could not speak or hide since

she found me, beneath the layers of poetry, a cover like a second skin of
plastic alphabet,

bleeding guns speechless

and then,

  somewhere

    I disappeared,

      becoming water

        under   her   tongue

NOTES

1. *Ghazal* is a genre of South Asian and West Asian mystical love poetry; *eshq-e-man* means my love; *mathnawi* is another kind of poem that was perfected by the poet Rumi; drupad is a classical vocal style in Indian music.
2. A classical raga is usually structured into three cohesive units. The *alap* is a slow introductory phase that spells out the specific notes and moods of the piece; Jor marks the crescendo of the music into a faster tempo, where the piece is developed; the *jhala* is the final section of the raga, where the music is played very fast until it reaches a climax and stops abruptly with the repetition of a significant set of notes, three times. The sentiment of the song is reflected by the raga, i.e. *malkauns* is a late night raga expressing desire for union with the beloved.
3. *Anjali* means offering
4. *Shanti jal* is holy water in Hindu rituals; *padmini* means lotus.
5. *Alpana* is a special decorative art, popular in Bengal, of painting intricate designs as adornment at the site of auspicious ceremonies.
6. *Madhur* means sweet.
7. *Mulaqat* means meeting.
8. *Rati* means sexual love.
9. *Mashuqa* is the female beloved.
10. *Bhairavi* is a sombre, pensive raga (classical Indian musical melody) that is ideally played in the morning. Each raga has a mood which is brought out most effectively at a particular time of day. While Bhairavi is best as a morning raga, Malkauns is a complex late night raga, marking the time when lovers meet.
11. *Sapno ki rani* means dream woman; *devi* means goddess; *kajal* is eyeliner, *bindi* is the decorative dot worn on the forehead by some South Asian women; *mehndi* is henna; *payal* is anklet; *Sati, Savitri, and Sita* are idealized female figures in Hindu iconography; *Radha-Krishna* are the archetypical lovers in Hinduism; *Kamala* was the prostitute, extraordinarily skilled in the art of love, who seduced Siddhartha before he attained enlightenment to become Buddha; *ashirbad* means blessing.
12. The first italicized passage in "Sound of a Heart Cracking" is my reworking of the following lines from "A Love Poem" by Catherine Manansala:

I've been searching for you in foreign
courtyards - seeking your murmur in language,
your stare in photographs, your breath in
strange breezes.
[...]

The way you arrange splendour
of limbs in darkness, whirl me through
cyclones of embrace,
I can find nowhere else.

13. *Kumkum* is the vermillion powder many women wear in the parting of their hair, signifying their married status; *mangalsutra* is a necklace worn also by married women.

14. *Draupadi* and *Chandrabhaga* are women from Indian epics and legends. *Surya* is the sun god, who actually raped Chandrabhaga, not knowing that she was his sister. The *Gayatri mantra* I include here ("Om....dayat") is ironically a popular prayer to Surya, invoking his blessings. *Satyam shivam sundaram* is a widely known phrase, meaning "truth, god, and beauty." The *Vedas* are ancient Hindu texts, *darshanas* are another set of religious texts, and *Sruti - Smriti* are categories of those texts, distinguishing "that which is heard" and "that which is remembered," respectively. *Vishnu* is the god who preserves creation by appearing in different incarnations to defeat evil in the world and so protect his devotees. *Buddha* and *Krishna* are said to be other forms of Vishnu.

15. Quotations used throughout this book are from the following poetic works:

Fariduddin Attar, *The Conference of the Birds,* translated from Persian by Afkham Darbandi and Dick Davis. Harmondsworth: Penguin Books, 1986.
Anne Carson, "The Book of Isaiah II," *Glass, Irony, and God.* New York: New Directions, 1995.
Lorna Goodison, "Mother the Great Stones Got to Move," *To Us All Flowers Are Roses.* Chicago: University of Illinois Press, 1995.
Pablo Neruda, *100 Love Sonnets,* translated from Spanish by Stephen Tapscott. Austin: University of Texas Press, 1986.
Michael Ondaatje, "Rock Bottom," *The Cinnamon Peeler: Selected Poems.* Toronto: MacLelland and Stewart Inc., 1989.
Adrienne Rich, "In the Wake of Home," *The Fact of a Doorframe: Poems Selected and New, 1950-1984.* New York: W.W. Norton and Company, 1984.
Jelaluddin Rumi, *Love is a Stranger*, translated from Persian by Kabir Edmund Helminski. Vermont: Threshold Books, 1993.
Rabindranath Tagore, *The Gardener*, translated from Bengali by the author himself. New York: The Macmillan Company, 1914.

Acknowledgments

For their grace and patience, I am indebted to my mother, Pubali, and my brother, Joy. I wish to thank Nicholas Boston and Faizal Deen, Maneesha Deckha, Anjula Gogia, Ahmar Husain, Marcia James, Devaki Panini, Harsha Ram, and Priya and Yana Watson for their enduring friendship and sustenance.

Jake Brown, Tisa Bryant, Michael Chervin, Karin Cope, Tanya Evanson, Marike Finlay-de Monchy, Salman Husain, Janet Lumb, Kristin Norget, Himmat Shinhat, Atif Siddiqui, George Szanto, Jade Williams, Tamara Vukov, and members of Saathi have all offered invaluable support and encouragement.

I am grateful to the Canada Council for the Arts for their financial assistance.

Shashin Parhami, thank you for the beautiful eye. Finally, a very special thanks to my father, Dilip K Banerji, for his generous heart and unfailing love.